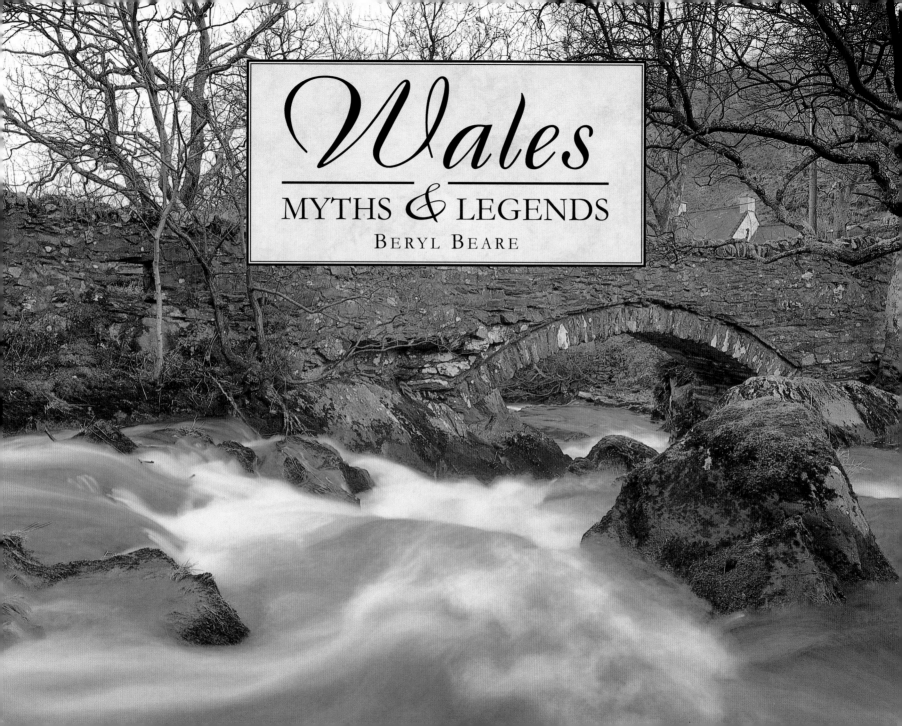

Wales

MYTHS & LEGENDS

BERYL BEARE

Wales

MYTHS & LEGENDS

Beryl Beare

SIENA

For John

A Siena book
Siena is an imprint of Parragon Books

First published in Great Britain in 1996 by
Parragon Books Limited
Units 13-17, Avonbridge Industrial Estate
Atlantic Road, Avonmouth, Bristol BS11 9QD
United Kingdom

Designed and produced by
Touchstone
Old Chapel Studio, Plain Road, Marden
Tonbridge, Kent TN12 9LS United Kingdom

© Parragon Books Limited 1996

ISBN 0-75251-699-X

Printed in Italy

Photographic credits:
(Abbreviations: r = right, l = left, t = top, b = below)

The Image Bank: 1, 2-3, 4, 5, 6-7, 8, 9, 10-11,
12, 14, 16*(t)*, 16-17, 20-21, 21*(r)*, 22*(b)*, 24-25,
26-27, 28*(b)*, 28-29, 29*(b)*, 30, 31, 32*(l)*, 33, 35,
36-37, 38, 39, 40*(r)*, 40*(l)*, 43, 45, 46-47, 47*(r)*,
49*(r)*, 50*(b)*, 51*(t)*, 54-55, 55*(b)*, 56, 59, 60, 61,
62*(t)*, 62*(b)*, 63, 64*(l)*, 65*(r)*, 65(l), 66*(b)*, 66-67,
68-69, 69*(r)*, 69*(l)*, 70, 74-75, 76, 77*(l)*, 77*(r)*, 79.

Greg Evans International: 11*(r)*, 13, 15*(b)*,
22-23, 50*(t)*, 52*(t)*, 52-53, 58, 72*(l)*, 72*(r)*, 73.

Telegraph Colour Library: 15*(t)*, 16*(b)*, 18-19,
32*(r)*, 37*(r)*, 41, 48-49, 52*(b)*, 57, 71, 78.

Colorific!: 18, 27*(b)*, 34-35, 42, 44, 50-51, 64*(r)*.

Special thanks to Claire Morgans at Bwrdd
Croeso Cymru – Wales Tourist Board.

Above: Celtic cross at Carew, Pembrokeshire.
*Opposite: The last of the winter snow on the Snowdon
Horseshoe in the early morning sunshine.*

Contents

Introduction

THE Welsh are justly proud of their Celtic past and the wealth of myths and legends that surround it. Wales itself is surely an enchanted land – or at least, it must come closer to enchantment than most!

It is a land of music, mystery and magic – qualities that are reflected time and again in its folklore. The legends were passed down by word of mouth from generation to generation, through the centuries. Stories of heroic deeds, brave warriors and romantic love – of monsters and magicians, witches and fairy folk. An intriguing galaxy that formed the folklore of Cymru (Wales).

Many of the legends are to be found in *The Mabinogion*, a collection of medieval Welsh tales. And, of course, Wales has a special claim to Arthur 'the once-and-future King' – a legend that has remained unchanged over the years. But was King Arthur a purely mythological character, or did he really exist as a leader of the Celts?

We are left wondering, and perhaps the mystery enhances the magic. The first written account of Arthur was in the 12th century, in Geoffrey of Monmouth's *History of the Kings of Britain*.

Giants and dragons feature prominently in Welsh folklore, particularly in the mountain regions. The name of the topmost peak of Snowdon, Yr Wyddfa, means 'the tomb' and is a legendary burial mound erected over a giant.

The rugged splendour and stern beauty of the mountain – where the first conquerors of Everest trained – provides an ideal setting for mythological monsters and legendary heroes. It also warns us that caution and respect are needed, for benevolent weather can change with lethal swiftness on any Welsh mountain.

In the mid-19th century, gold mining was a feature of Wales. The yield was sufficient at Clogau mine, west of Cwm Mynach, to turn Dolgellau into a small-scale Dawson City. This mine was the source of the gold that is used for royal wedding rings.

Now the gold mines are closed, but legendary treasure aplenty lies hidden in hill, cave and lake – along with the odd giant, dragon and water-monster!

Traditionally, fairy folk have their own gold. But they seem more willing to share their magical treasures – particularly their healing skills – to which end they allocate their time with care. It was said in Elizabethan Wales that soothsayers, enchanters and physicians claimed to walk with the fairies on Tuesday and Thursday nights.

Right: Iced water on the edge of a lake at dusk in the wild and beautiful Snowdonia National Park.

Legends from Anglesey

The Cairn of Branwen

Bedd Branwen, Llanbabo, Gwynedd

BRAN, THE giant king of the Island of the Mighty (Britain), was sitting with one of his brothers on the rock of Harlech, when they saw ships approaching from Ireland. They belonged to the Irish king, Matholwch, and he had come to ask for the hand of their sister, Branwen.

The request was well received, permission was given for the marriage and a wedding feast arranged. It was a very grand affair, no expense was spared and the guests were obviously enjoying themselves.

Unfortunately, the celebrations were brought to an untimely end by Efnisien – one of Bran's younger brothers – when he insulted the Irish king, who promptly stormed out of the court.

Seeking to appease Matholwych, Bran offered him his most treasured possession, the Cauldron of Rebirth – a magic cauldron that restored the dead to life. The Irish king accepted the gift and sailed back to Ireland with his new bride.

For a year Branwen was held in high regard at the Irish court and lived happily. Then her husband, who had not forgiven her brother's conduct, divorced her and put her to work in the palace kitchens.

Branwen endured this slavery for three years, but meantime trained a starling to carry a message to her brother, Bran.

The giant king immediately launched an invasion of Ireland. Too big to board a ship himself, he carried many of his men across the river Shannon on his massive shoulders.

A cruel and bloody war took place, in which the Irish put the magic cauldron to use and restored their dead to fight another day. Then Efnisien – perhaps seeking to make amends for the trouble he had started in the first place – successfully put an end to the cauldron's magical powers by willing his heart to burst while he was inside it.

Bran himself was mortally wounded in the foot by a poisoned spear. He ordered his followers to cut off his head when he died, bear it back to Britain and bury it in London, with its face towards France. The head was buried where the Tower of London now stands.

Sadly, Branwen died of grief soon after, and seven warriors buried her on the Isle of Anglesey. Today, a ruined cairn near Llanbabo, on the banks of the River Alaw, is said to mark her grave.

Above: The eastern entrance to the Menai Strait which separates Anglesey from the mainland.

Right: Caernarfon Castle commands impressive views across the Menai Strait to the Isle of Anglesey.

The Giantess's Apronful

Barclodiad y Gawres, Gwynedd

ONCE, WHEN the land was still young, there were two giants – a husband and wife – who wanted to build themselves a new house on the Isle of Anglesey.

They set off, taking with them a number of stones. The husband carried a large stone under each arm, intended for the door-frame of the house, and his wife carried a quantity of smaller rocks in her apron.

As they travelled, they met a cobbler and asked him the way. He pointed them in the direction of Anglesey and the giantess, who had aching feet, asked how far it was.

The cobbler liked to tease, so he pointed to all the shoes he was carrying to be repaired and said solemnly, 'I have already worn out all these shoes walking from there!'

The giant gave a groan and dropped his two large boulders. The giantess was even more dismayed and threw up her arms in horror, emptying the contents of her apron on to the ground.

The rocks are still there, on the headland above Porth Trecastell Bay. They are called Barclodiad y Gawres – 'The Giantess's Apronful'.

Right: Dinas Dinlle beach on the Lleyn Peninsula.

The Robber's Stone

Carreg y Lleider, Gwynedd

THERE is a standing stone in a field south of Llandyfrydog that looks like a man with a pack on his back. It is known as Carreg y Lleider – 'The Robber's Stone'.

The country people say it is a thief who stole books from a local church. As he crossed the field, with the sack containing the holy booty on his back, he was turned to stone.

There he remains, petrified and unmoving – except for once every year. When the clock strikes twelve on Christmas Eve, the stone is said to move three times round the field in which it stands.

The Blue Horse

Cemaes Bay, Gwynedd

MANY YEARS ago, a young man who lived near the bay had a violent row with his family. He mounted his dappled blue-grey horse and galloped furiously away from home.

He was so blinded by rage that he rode his horse right over the cliff-edge. His body was never found, but the carcass of the blue-grey horse was discovered, washed into the cave at Cemaes Bay. Ever since that time it has been called Ogof y March Glas – the cave of the blue horse.

Above: Penrhyn Castle, Gwynedd.

The Druids of Anglesey

Cemaes Bay, Gwynedd

THE DRUID priests were very powerful among the Celts, and much of their activity in North Wales seems to have been centred on Anglesey.

It is hardly surprising that so little is known of Druid history, for they were very protective about their beliefs – and their religion forbade the use of the written word. We do know that some of the Druid rites were horrific, and included placing people in wickerwork cages and burning them to death as gifts to the gods.

The Roman invaders descended on Anglesey in 61AD and – most unusually – were thrown into temporary disarray when they first saw the Druid forces. The sight of white robed figures raising sacrificial swords to heaven and uttering terrible incantations was something the Romans had never encountered before, and at first their casualties were many.

Roman military discipline soon prevailed, however, and they managed to reorganize their forces and counter-attack.

The Druids were soon defeated, but they seem to have continued a form of guerrilla warfare. There are tales of white clad priests swinging from trees with their curved knives, and beheading Romans who were destroying the sacred forests of Anglesey.

The Deadly Viper

Penhesgyn, near Penmynydd, Gwynedd

THERE WAS a prophet living on the Isle of Anglesey who was greatly respected by the people. One day, he prophesied that a great viper would soon come to Penhesgyn and kill the heir to the family fortune.

The family, fearing for their son's safety, sent him to England to cheat his fate.

Shortly after the young man's departure a huge viper did, in fact, arrive at Penhesgyn. The local men quickly dug a pit in a field and covered it with a brass vessel that gleamed in the sun, to attract the creature.

It was not long before the viper slithered towards the trap and was attacked by the men. They hacked it to death and buried it in the pit.

The danger being over, the young heir was summoned home, and straightaway demanded to see the creature that had intended to kill him. When it was dug up, and he saw the ugly head for the first time, he kicked it in contempt.

The viper, however, was still deadly after death. Its fang pierced the young man's foot and poisoned him, so that he died just as the prophet had foretold.

Right: Beaumaris Castle with its views across to the mainland and to the north.
Left: Legend suggests that Caernarfon castle was built as a wedding gift for a beautiful bride.

Snowdonia

The Haunted Island

Bardsey Island, Gwynedd

IN THE early Middle Ages Bardsey was known as 'the gate of Paradise'. Spiritually, three pilrimages to Bardsey Abbey – now a ruin – were considered equal to one journey to Rome.

Now only a handful of people live on this bleak and haunted little island off the Lleyn peninsula. But 20,000 monks are reputed to be buried there, and Merlin is said to be sleeping in a cave surrounded by treasure, to awake only when King Arthur returns once more to defend his country.

However, another legend says that Merlin still lives on the island in an invisible house of glass.

In the house with him are ancient magical objects, known as the Thirteen Treasures of Britain. They include a cloak of invisibility, a chariot that enables the traveller to arrive instantly at any destination, a chess set that plays by itself – and a sword that bursts into flames when it is drawn.

Merlin also has the true throne of Britain, and when Arthur returns the faithful magician will bring it out and enthrone him. Meanwhile, ghosts in cowls pace along Bardsey beach when shipwrecks are imminent.

The Faithful Hound

Beddgelert, Gwynedd

LLEWELLYN the Great, a 12th century prince of Wales, lived in a village at the foot of Snowdon. He owned many fine hunting dogs, but his favourite animal was a gentle and intelligent hound named Gelert.

One day, Llewellyn and his wife went hunting, leaving Gelert to guard their baby son. When they returned from the chase, Gelert bounded to greet his master. But Llewellyn saw that the dog's muzzle was covered in blood.

In the centre of the room was the baby's crib, overturned and with blood trickling from beneath it. Llewellyn gave a cry of despair, and believing the dog to have killed his son, thrust his sword deep into Gelert's side.

As the hound lay dying, Llewellyn heard a whimpering from the crib. Lifting it, he discovered the baby lying on the floor, completely unharmed. Nearby, partly hidden by bloodstained linen, was the mutilated body of a wolf.

Gelert had killed the wolf and saved the child, only to die at the hands of his master. Filled with remorse, Llewellyn raised a tomb over the faithful hound, and this became known as Beddgelert, or 'Gelert's Grave'.

Above: Clouds gather dramatically over the mountains.

Left: Sunset off the Lleyn peninsular.

Right: The old bridge at Beddgelert.

The Afanc

Betws-y-Coed, Gwynedd

Above: The powerful Swallow Falls at Betws-y-Coed.

THE AFANC is a fearful monster that defies description. Years ago, one lived in a pool called Llyn yr Afanc, above Betws-y-Coed. It had magical powers and was causing floods that drowned cattle and ruined crops, and the local people were in despair.

Then Hu Gadarn came to their rescue with his two mighty oxen, and agreed to drag the Afanc away. But how was the creature to be reached? It lurked in the deepest part of the pool where no one dare venture.

Eventually, a lovely maiden was persuaded to entice it out, and while the others hid themselves, she sat on the bank and sang a lilting melody. It was not long before the terrible monster surfaced and lumbered out of the pool, to rest its ugly great head in her lap.

Hu Gadarn and his helpers rushed forward and threw chains round the creature. It bellowed with rage and sprang up, injuring the maiden with its great taloned claw as it did so.

The chains held, however, and the oxen dragged the Afanc to the waters of Llyn Glaslyn, on Mount Snowdon, where it is said to swim to this day.

Above and right: The seasonal beauty of Cader Idris.

The Bottomless Pool

Cader Idris, Gwynedd

CADER IDRIS means 'Idris's Chair' and, in legend, Idris was a giant. In reality, however, he was more likely to have been a Celtic chieftain who died fighting the Saxon invaders.

The great mountain of Cader Idris spreads itself for some 10 miles across north-west Wales, dividing the old territory of Gwynedd from the land of Powys. Towards the summit, to the south-east, is the reputedly bottomless pool of Llyn Cau, the 'shut in lake'. It is held in a huge rock-enclosed bowl, scooped from the slopes of Cader Idris by an Ice Age glacier.

In the dark still waters of Llyn Cau a monster is said to live, appearing only to devour those who venture in to the pool.

Some people believe that the presence of the monster was established in the 18th century, when a youth was dared to swim in Llyn Cau. Rashly, he accepted the dare, and plunged into the pool. As he swam towards the centre he suddenly disappeared beneath the surface of the water, and was never seen again.

It is also said that anyone who sleeps by Llyn Cau will awake blind, mad – or a poet.

The Two Dragons

Dinas Emrys, Beddgelert, Gwynedd

IN THE fifth century, the Celtic King Vortigern was hard pressed by invading Saxons and decided to build a fort in Snowdonia.

He chose a domed shape hill near Beddgelert and set his royal masons to work. They started with a good heart, but the following morning discovered that all their building materials had mysteriously vanished.

The same thing happened on the following morning, and again the next morning; on each occasion the materials had simply disappeared overnight. Angry and frustrated, Vortigern consulted his magicians. They told him he would only be successful if he sprinkled the foundations with the blood of a boy born without a father.

Such a 'Wonderchild' – born of a human mother and Otherworld father – was a boy known as Myrddin, who lived close by. He was duly brought before the king, and made ready for the sacrifice.

Now Myrddin was, in fact, Merlin the magician who possessed a great many magical powers and had the gift of vision. He told the king that the foundations of his fort were being undermined by a subterranean lake, in which two dragons lay sleeping.

Vortigern's own magicians advised him to ignore the boy's words and carry out the sacrifice as planned. But Vortigern was uncertain. Eventually he decided to heed the boy, and had his labourers dig deep beneath the foundations.

The underground lake was there, just as Myrddin had said. Orders were given for it to be drained, and two sleeping dragons were discovered – one white and one red.

The dragons awoke and began to fight. The battle was long and bloody, for the beasts were well matched, but finally, the red dragon was victorious, and the white dragon turned and fled.

Myrddin explained that the white dragon represented the Saxons and the red dragon represented the Welsh, who in the fullness of time would reconquer their lands. It is said that this was how the Red Dragon became a symbol of Wales and found its way on to the Welsh flag.

Vortigern's fort was completed without further misadventure. Myrddin then revealed his true identity to the king, telling him that he was Merlin, also known as Emrys. And to show his gratitude, Vortigern named the fort Dinas Emrys.

Left: Nantgwynant, near Beddgelert.
Far Left: The ruins of Castell y Bere, Gwynedd.

The Town That Drowned

Lake Bala, Gwynedd

WHAT IS now Llyn Tegid – Lake Bala – was once a valley in which there was a town. The nobleman who ruled this community was one of the cruelest and most depraved men in Wales. His friends and relatives were little better.

When his first son was born, he held a lavish party at the palace, and engaged a local harpist to play at the feast. The young harpist detested the nobleman and his friends, but knew it would be unwise to refuse.

On the night of the feast the drunken guests ignored his playing and the party grew ever wilder. Suddenly, the harpist heard a low whisper behind him and turning, saw a small bluebird. 'Follow me!' it whispered urgently. 'Follow me!'

The harpist left the palace unnoticed and followed the bluebird to the top of a hill. Then, mysteriously, the little creature disappeared.

Feeling rather foolish, the young man decided to sleep. When he awoke at dawn he looked down to the valley and, to his amazement, saw a huge lake.

There was no trace of the town or the people at all – only his harp floating on the surface of the water.

Right: The mysterious Lake Bala.

The Strongest Woman

Llanberis, Gwynedd

IT IS SAID that the strongest woman to have lived in Wales was born at Llanberis, and died at the turn of the 18th century aged 105 years. At the age of 70 she could still out-wrestle any man in Wales.

She received many offers of marriage – her suitors probably considering it more prudent to have her as a wife than an adversary. In fairness, she did have many accomplishments and was an excellent musician, fiddle-maker, tailor, cobbler and carpenter.

From among her suitors she finally chose the smallest and puniest man. They say that she beat him twice, and that after the first beating he married her and after the second he became ardently religious.

The Moving Image

Llanderfel, Gwynedd

THE SHRINE of St Derfel contained a wooden image of the saint, the head and limbs of which moved mechanically.

The saint was reputed to have been one of King Arthur's warriors, and many pilgrims visited the shrine. It was believed, also, that the image could save condemned souls from hell.

During the Reformation it was taken to London and burnt, and a monk who refused to deny its miraculous powers was burnt with it. However, St Derfel's wooden horse remained in Llanderfel church.

Right: Llanberis, with Mount Snowdon in the distance.

The Devil's Tree

Llandudno, Gwynedd

THE REMAINS of an old oak tree on the Llanrhos Road, near Llandudno, is reputed to have belonged to the Devil.

At one time no horse would pass it without rearing violently. And a headless coachman who haunts the road was said to have been decapitated by a low-hanging branch from the tree.

A cobbler from Glan Conwy had been drinking at a tavern one night and was making his way along Llanrhos Road. Being deep in his cups, he did not keep to the other side of the road as usual, but passed right by the Devil's Tree, shouting abuse at it.

Suddenly, something hairy landed on his shoulder, gripping him tightly by the throat. Unable to dislodge the creature or cry out he stumbled on, hoping to meet someone who could help him.

He met no one, but after a terrifying walk managed to reach the village of Tywyn and struggled, half dead, to a friend's house. As the door was thrown open the weight left his shoulder and he fainted with relief.

His friend did not see the monster, but was mystified by the scorch marks on his friend's throat.

Below: Little Orme, Llandudno.

The Devil Returns

Llanfor, Gwynedd

THE DEVIL took a liking to the little village of Llanfor and was a frequent visitor, usually appearing in the form of a pig. No one was sure how to put a stop to his unwelcome visits until, eventually, the parson managed to subdue him.

He recited the service of exorcism while walking three times round his church, and in this way the Devil was rendered helpless. He was bound in chains and taken to a pool – now called Llyn y Goulan Goch – in the River Dee. There he would remain as long as an ancient lamp, hidden in the church, was kept burning.

The villagers celebrated joyfully. But unfortunately no one remembered to fill the lamp, and it went out.

The Devil returned in the form of a gentleman in a three-cornered hat, and constantly shouted interruptions during the church services.

Two magicians combined magical forces and managed to subdue him again. He was carried away and once more thrown into the pool. This time his stay would be longer, however, for he must remain there until he had counted every grain of sand at the bottom of the pool.

Left: Llyn Mymbyr, Snowdonia National Park.

Midwife to the Fairies

Llandwrog, Gwynedd

MANY YEARS ago, an old woman who had only one eye lived at Llandwrog. This is the story of how she came to lose the other eye.

One day, she went to Caernarfon with her husband to hire a servant and selected a girl with yellow hair. Her name was Eilian, and she duly arrived to take up her duties with the old couple.

On winter evenings she would go into the meadow to do her spinning by moonlight, and the fairies would visit her and sing and dance as she worked. Then one day in the spring she ran off with the fairies, and no more was heard of her.

Some time after, when the moon was full, a gentleman on horseback arrived at the old couple's door. He asked the old woman, who was known locally as a midwife, if she would come to his lady. She agreed, and rode pillion behind him to Rhos-y-Cowrt.

On the moor was an ancient fort, which they entered and were immediately inside a magnificent palace room. The old woman had never seen such a splendid place in her life.

The young wife lay in bed and was soon delivered of a fine baby boy. When the old woman had dressed the baby by the fire, the husband gave her some ointment with which to anoint its eyes. At the same time he warned her not to get any of it into her own.

However, the old woman accidentally rubbed one of her eyes with the finger she had used to apply the ointment. Immediately, she saw that the room was just a cave, the bed a mere pile of stones heaped with bracken, and the wife was none other than her servant girl, Eilian. Yet, with the other eye, she still saw the splendid room of the palace.

Shortly after this, the old woman went to Caernarfon market and saw the husband. She greeted him and asked, 'how is Eilian?'

'She is very well, thank you,' he replied, 'but with what eye do you see me?'

'With this one,' she said, pointing.

At once, the husband took a bulrush and poked the eye out. And that is how the old woman at Lladwrog came to have only one eye.

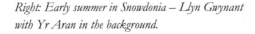

Right: Early summer in Snowdonia – Llyn Gwynant with Yr Aran in the background.

'Looking Them Dead'

Llyn Cwynch, Gwynedd

IN WELSH folklore, snakes and dragons are related creatures. And certainly the dragon who lived in the waters of Llyn Cwynch, east of Llanelltyd, had the paralyzing gaze of a snake.

No one was able to kill the creature, because it had the power of 'looking them dead'. Several brave men ventured forth with swords, determined to rid the countryside of this monster. But from whichever direction they approached, it always turned its head and killed them instantly with a glance.

At dawn one morning, a shepherd who saw the dragon from a distance observed that it appeared agitated and lowered its head when a cock crowed. The shepherd therefore armed himself with a sharp sword and a lively cockerel and made his way to Llyn Cwych.

Just before he was within looking distance from the dragon, he released the cockerel. As the bird flapped in front of it, the monster cringed and again lowered its head. The shepherd immediately decapitated it with his sword, and he and the cockerel returned home in triumph.

A cairn called Carnedd-y-Wiber, Cairn of the Serpent, still marks the spot where the dragon was slain.

Right: Winter thaw – the beautiful Llyn Gwynant.

The Floating Island

Llyn Dywarchen, Nantlle Valley, Gwynedd

LLYN DYWARCHEN – Lake of the Turf Sod – once had a legendary floating island. It was believed to be the meeting place of a mortal man who had married a water-fairy.

When the fairy returned to the lake, she was condemned never to to walk upon the earth again. And her husband, being mortal, was unable to visit her in her lakeland home. The island 'belonging neither to the earth nor the water' was the only place where they could meet.

A 12th century writer, Giraldus Cambrensis, referred to the island as floating backwards and forwards across the lake. He observed that cattle occasionally stepped on to it, chewed the grass for a while, and stepped off again when it next came close to the bank.

The 17th century astronomer Halley – who discovered the comet named after him – visited the lake, and was so intrigued by the legend that he decided to test it. He swam out to the island and found it did indeed float, and that he was able to steer it around the lake with a wooden paddle.

There is a large island in Dywarchen today – but it has never been known to float.

Below: Most Welsh lakes can boast their very own legend.

The Murdered Prince

Llyn Idwal, Gwynedd

LLYN IDWAL is surrounded by mountains and overlooked by an awesome cleft known as the Devil's Kitchen. But the lake has its own legend, which goes back some 800 years.

A prince of Gwynedd had a son called Idwal, of whom he was very proud. The boy was an exemplary scholar, although it was obvious that he did not have the makings of a warrior.

When his father engaged in warfare with King Hywel of Powys, the boy was sent to stay with his uncle Neffyd, who lived on the banks of a secluded lake. This uncle had a son called Rhun, who was as dull and graceless as Idwal was clever and charming.

Now Nefydd was both vain and jealous, and could not bear to see his son comparing so unfavourably with the young prince. He told Rhun to take Idwal for a walk around the lake and when they came to a particularly deep part, to push him in.

Idwal regarded his cousin as a friend and was happy to accompany him on a walk. So when he felt himself pushed in to the icy water, he must have thought it was an accident.

Spluttering and struggling for breath, he called to Rhun for help. And the last thing he saw before he drowned was his cousin laughing at him from the bank.

Idwal's father was distraught and banished Nefydd and his family from the kingdom. He decreed that the lake should be named after his son – Llyn Idwal, or 'Idwal's Lake'.

All the birds fled the lake in sorrow after the young prince's murder. They have returned to the shores since, but it is unlikely that you will see any of them fly over the lake – for they took a vow never to do so again.

Above: Mount Tryfan from near Devil's Kitchen.

Right: Llyn Ogwen is reputed to contain buried treasure and may be the lake into which King Arthur hurled his legendary sword – Excalibur.

The Lake of Buried Treasures

Llyn Ogwen, Gwynedd

CLOUD-CAPPED mountains watch over the shallow waters of Llyn Ogwen, a lake of many legends.

Tryfan, one of the mountains towering above the lake, is said to be the burial place of Sir Bedivere, the last of King Arthur's knights. And Ogwen is one of the possible lakes in to which Arthur might have thrown his sword, Excalibur.

Many years ago, a great landslide from Tryfan fell into the lake, and is reputed to have buried a cave containing the most fabulous treasures.

Above: Could this be the burial place of Sir Bedivere?

The Lake of the Maidens

Llyn Morynion, Gwynedd

MANY YEARS ago, three young men set out in search of wives. They came from an area where there were very few women and had heard that the Vale of Clwyd was known for its attractive maidens.

They arrived at their destination after two days travel on horseback, and set up camp in the Vale. Then they started the serious business of stalking and capturing their prey. Whenever they found a suitable young woman on her own, they seized her, tied her up and took her back to their camp.

Soon they had three desirable but struggling captives who wailed and screamed and begged to be released. The young men seemed genuinely surprised by the girls' reaction, and assured them that they meant no harm and could promise them a good life.

They bundled the young women on to their horses and started the journey home. Soon the girls realized that their captors were not evil at all, but three friendly and charming youths – even if their approach to courtship was somewhat unorthodox.

As they journeyed, the young men told the girls all about their village and how welcome they would be there. The girls began to relax and talked about their own lives. Each admitted that she had endured a particularly strict upbringing and was not altogether sorry to be leaving home.

By evening the girls had been untied and were accompanying their future husbands quite willingly. They camped overnight on the banks of a mountain lake, and in the morning the men made a fire while the women prepared breakfast.

Later, they all bathed together in the lake, and as they were laughing and splashing each other, several riders appeared from the forest. The youths saw that they were armed with swords and axes and ran for their own weapons. But they were too late. The riders overtook them and brutally hacked them to death.

The girls then recognized the attackers as their fathers and brothers. Horrified, and distraught at the loss of their new found loves, they ran back into the lake and drowned themselves.

Ever since that day, the little lake above Ffestiniog has been called Llyn Morynion – 'the Lake of the Maidens'.

Right: Snowdon overlooks Llyn Mymbyr at sunset.
Below: The blue waters of Llyn Padarn, Gwynedd.

The Good Giant Twrog

Maentwrog, Gwynedd

THE VILLAGE of Maentwrog is a few miles from the slate town of Ffestiniog. Maen Twrog means 'St Twrog's Stone', and by the porch in the churchyard is a stone of unknown origin.

It is said that a giant called Twrog once lived in the district. He was on a nearby hill one day, when he saw pagan rites being performed in a field where the church now stands. From the hill-top, he threw a stone which destroyed the pagan altar. His followers then built a church where the stone had become imbedded in the ground.

To this day, you can still see the marks of Twrog's thumb and fingers on the stone.

The Tall Stones

Y Meini Hirion, Gwynedd

AMONG A collection of stones above Penmaenmawr stand the 'Deity Stone' and the 'Stone of Sacrifice'.

It is claimed that if anyone swears near the Deity Stone, it will lean forward and strike them. And the Stone of Sacrifice, like the giant Twrog, appears to be intolerant of pagan ceremonies.

Witches were in the habit of gathering at the stone circle to perform such ceremonies. One night the Stone of Sacrifice shouted out a warning to them to cease, whereupon two of the witches died of fright on the spot!

Left: View from Great Orem towards Penmaenmawr.
Below: An aerial view of the fantasy village, Portmerion.

The Fantasy Village

Portmeirion, Gwynedd

PORTMEIRION is the result of an ambitious project by Sir Clough William-Ellis, an architect and descendant of Cynan, Prince of Gwynedd, who built Castle Deuraeth here in the 12th century.

William-Ellis bought Aba Ia – 'Frozen Estuary' – in 1925 and made a seaside town from everything he liked best, to create what he called his 'light opera approach to architecture'. There are Georgian looking houses, a Jacobean county hall and a Pantheon with an ornate Victorian facade. Many other bits and pieces were used if he thought they fitted in – including a giant Buddha left over from a film set.

Portmerion is probably best known to many people as the setting for the cult television series *The Prisoner*, in which it represented a mystery security village that might have been anywhere.

Early in the 19th century the monstrous 'Hwntw Mawr', a notorious murderer, lived in a cottage in Aber Ia.

He robbed a farm just above the hamlet and murdered a servant girl who tried to resist him. He then attempted to escape across the sands, but was caught and publicly hanged at Dolgelly in April, 1813.

Left: Portmerion village captures the imagination.

Elen of the Regions

Sarn Helen, Gwynedd

SARN HELEN means 'Helen's Street' (or 'Elen's Street'), and refers to the great Roman road that runs below the fort at Tomen-y-Mur. Many Roman roads in Wales are called by the same name, but this one is particularly associated with the legendary Elen of the Regions – or Elen of the Hosts.

One day, the Roman Emperor Macsen was out hunting and lay down to sleep in the noonday heat. He dreamt that he sailed to a distant land, where he found himself among mountains and saw a great castle at a river mouth.

He entered the castle and was greeted by a girl, who invited him to sit beside her on her golden throne. But just as he was about to take her in his arms, he was awakened by the noise of the hunt.

Macsen was so in love with the girl that he began to neglect his empire. His counsellors suggested that he sent messengers to look for the castle, which he did. After a year of searching in vain, the messengers came to Wales and discovered a castle at the mouth of the River Seint.

They found the girl inside the castle, just as their emperor had described her. But when they told her of Macsen's dream she was sceptical. 'I neither doubt what you tell me,' she said, 'nor do I overmuch believe it.'

She refused to accompany them to Rome to marry Macsen. 'If he loves me,' she said, 'let him come to me!'

So Macsen came to Caernarfon in Wales and married the girl, who was, of course, Elen. As a wedding gift she asked for three strongholds to be built – at Caernarfon, Caerleon and Carmarthen.

After the forts had been built, Elen gave instructions for roads to be made from one stronghold to another. And these roads came to be called the Roads of Elen of the Hosts.

Macsen enjoyed seven years happiness with his lovely bride in Caernarfon, but then a usurper arose in Rome and he returned there with his legions. Elen's brothers with their warriors went too, and it was they who retook the Roman city for Macsen.

In fact, Macsen was likely to have been Maximus Magnus, a Spanish born soldier who served in the Roman army in Britain in the fourth century.

Far Left: The Nantgynant Valley, Caernarfon, remains beautiful and unspoilt.
Below: Harlech Castle stands majestically on the hillside.

The Cloak of Beards

Snowdon, Gwynedd

A LEGENDARY giant was buried beneath a cairn on the highest peak of Snowdon – Yr Wyddfa. In the 19th century the cairn was known as Carnedd y Cawr – the 'Giant's Cairn' – until it was removed to make way for an hotel.

The giant, whose name was Rhita, was reputed to have made a cloak from the beards of all the kings he had slain. However, he felt the cloak was incomplete without the beard of King Arthur, and therefore sent a message requesting Arthur to send his beard.

As Arthur was more famous than the other kings, he offered to sew his beard higher on the cloak than all the rest. But if Arthur should refuse, he challenged him to a combat on Snowdon, the winner to take both the cloak and the beard of his defeated opponent.

Arthur refused to send his beard, but accepted the challenge, and presented himself on the summit of Snowdon at the appointed time.

Rhita's strength and size were enormous, but Arthur's skill was unsurpassed. Finally, he managed to slay the giant and take possession of the extraordinary cloak.

Right: The last of the winter snow lingers on the magnificent peaks of Snowdon and Y Lliwedd.

The Pass of Arrows

Snowdon, Gwynedd

KING ARTHUR is said to have fought his last battle below Snowdon's summit, at Bwlch y Saethau – the 'Pass of the Arrows'.

Medraut, another Briton, had insulted Arthur's beautiful queen, Guinevere. Arthur retaliated by raiding Medraut's home, and this led to the fatal last battle.

As King Arthur led his knights through the pass, to the summit of Snowdon, a great hail of arrows met them and the legendary king fell, mortally wounded.

His body was covered with stones to form a cairn, which is still there today and is known as Carnedd Arthur – 'Arthur's Cairn'.

The Mount of Eagles

Snowdon, Gwynedd

FOR MANY years, the eagles of Snowdon were regarded as oracles of fortune or disaster. In time of war, if they circled high over the summit of the mountain it was said to bode well, and meant that victory was near. But if they flew low over the rocks it was a sign that the Welsh would be defeated.

If they should cry incessantly, it was taken as a warning of some forthcoming calamity. The birds, it seemed, were mourning the event before it occurred.

Right: The beautiful autumn colours of Snowdonia.

The Flower Maiden

Tomen-y-Mur, Gwynedd

MATH THE magician was a lord of Gwynedd and had a son called Lleu Llaw Gyffes, 'Bright one of the Skilful Hand'. But the boy's mother would have nothing to do with him – other than putting a curse upon him so that he could never wed a mortal woman.

Math was determined that his son should marry, and when the time came he and Lleu made a maiden from flowers. They took the flowers of the oak, the broom and the meadowsweet, and they conjured the most beautiful woman ever seen. They gave her the name of Blodeuedd, the Welsh for 'Flowers'.

Lleu took Blodeuedd to his court at Mur Castell (Tomen-y-Mur) and they lived very happily for a time. Then, one day Blodeuedd met Gronw, lord of Penllyn and the two of them fell in love and plotted together to kill Lleu.

Lleu, however, could only be slain under certain conditions, 'neither within a house nor without, neither on foot nor on horseback, and the weapon a poisoned spear that has been one year in the making'.

A year later, Gronw had made the poisoned spear and Blodeuedd prepared a bath for Lleu on the river-bank, with a thatched roof overhead – 'neither within nor without'. By the tub she tethered a goat, and Lleu placed one foot on the goat and the other on the tub – 'neither on foot nor on horseback'. At that precise moment Gronw shot him with the poisoned spear, and

Lleu gave a terrible shriek and rose into the air in the form of an eagle.

Blodeuedd and Gronw settled at Mur Castell, but meantime Gwydion – nephew to Math the magician – was searching throughout Wales for Lleu. He found him in the Nantlle Valley below Snowdon and restored his human form to him. Then they both set out to seek revenge.

Blodeuedd fled with her maidens, but as they crossed the moors the maidens looked back in fear, stumbled and fell into a lake, where they all drowned.

Blodeuedd was caught on the bank of the lake by Gwydion, who used his magic to turn her into an owl – to be so hated by the other birds that she could only come out at night.

Above: Snowdon from the Nantlle Valley.

Right: Reflections of Llyn Gwynant on a misty morning.

Legends of Clwyd

The Bloody Hand

Chirk, Clwyd

CHIRK CASTLE is two miles outside the village of Chirk (Y Waun) and has been occupied by the Myddleton family since 1595. The family arms included a red hand, and this was the traditional 'bloody hand' put there to remind them of past misdeeds.

According to legend, it could not be removed until a prisoner survived 10 years in the castle dungeons. But the harshness of the dungeons took its toll very rapidly and few prisoners survived for long.

One prisoner did seem about to rid the Myddleton family of its gruesome symbol, for he survived almost the full 10 years. The dungeons must have defeated him in the end, however, for the red hand remains on the arms to this day.

The Gap of the Graves

Chirk, Clwyd

NEAR CHIRK Castle there are still traces of Offa's Dyke, the rampart built in the eighth century by Offa, King of Mercia.

A gap in the dyke is known as Adwy'r Beddau – 'the Gap of the Graves'. Here, in the 12th century, King Henry II of England was defeated by the Welsh, for this is the traditional site of the Battle of Crogen.

Above and right: Offa's Dyke runs between Prestatyn in the north and Chepstow in the south.
Far Right: From rolling hills to rugged mountains, the beautiful Welsh countryside is rich and varied.

Sir John of the Thumbs

Denbigh, Clwyd

MANY YEARS AGO the town of Denbigh was terrorized by a dragon. It had taken up residence in the ruined castle and darted out to make a meal of cattle and sheep – and even shepherds. It obviously enjoyed the local cuisine because it foraged for food more and more frequently, until no one was safe.

Among the townsfolk was a knight called Sion Bodiau – 'Sir John of the Thumbs' – who had two thumbs on each hand. The local people thought this must surely give him the power to deal with a dragon, and urged him to approach the castle.

Now Sir John was neither particularly brave, nor was he endowed with magic powers. But looking back at the angry widows of the town, he had little choice. Trembling, he went towards the dragon's lair.

The dragon, as would be expected, charged out of its castle breathing fire. Then it suddenly halted, staring down at the shivering knight's hands in amazement. Sir John immediately seized his opportunity, raised his sword and quickly beheaded the creature.

'Dim Bych! Dim Bych!' ('no more dragon') the townsfolk shouted joyfully. And Dinbych, the Welsh name for Denbigh, is still pronounced as 'Dim-bych' by the locals.

Castle of Mystery

Dinas Bran, Clwyd

ABOVE THE Vale of Llangollen, a hill-fort with Iron Age ramparts encloses the remains of a medieval castle – Dinas Bran, or 'Bran's stronghold'. This castle is possibly the most mysterious place in Arthurian legend, The Castle of the Grail.

In the 15th century, the Castle of the Grail was called 'Corbin', an old French word for crow. In fact, 'Bran' also means crow, and three centuries later Dinas Bran was referred to as 'Crow Castle'.

It was once claimed that Bran kept a buried treasure in the castle. By some mysterious means the castle was burnt and the country round about laid waste. Only one knight survived and people came from far and wide to see the wonders of the place. The blackened teeth of the ruined castle walls against a blood-red sunset were a grim and impressive sight.

A later legend attributes the burying of the treasure to Merlin, the magician. It was said that the finder of the hidden treasure would be the person he intended it for – a yellow-haired boy followed by a dog with light eyes, 'such as were said to see the wind'.

The Disappearance

Greenfield, Clwyd

A STRANGE legend tells of a 12th century monk from Basingwerk Abbey who heard a nightingale singing in a nearby wood. Entranced by the beautiful melody, he remained listening to it for what seemed like hours.

When he returned to the abbey, he found it in ruins and yet there was no sign of any disaster. To his further amazement, all the people around him were strangers. He asked what had happened, but no one seemed to understand him.

Then one woman remarked that his sudden appearance reminded her of an old story of another monk, who had disappeared suddenly many centuries before.

The villagers offered the bewildered holy man some refreshment – but as soon as he touched the food, he crumbled to dust.

The Devil's Splash

Llanddulas, Clwyd

THE DEVIL once lived in a cave on Pen y Cefyn mountain, and when the good people of Llanddulas could stand him no longer, they held a service of exorcism outside his cave .

During the service a loud splash was heard as the Devil fell into a deep, muddy pool. And that is why he's been black ever since – but he's never bothered the good folk of Llanddulas again.

Left: Castell Dinas, Llangollen.

Above: Rich with myths and legends, the Clwydian Range, viewed from the Vale of Clwyd.

The Cursing Well

Llaneilian-yn-Rhos, Clwyd

THE VILLAGE of Llaneilian-yn-Rhos, near Colwyn Bay, was famous for its cursing well. All that was needed to inflict ill-fortune on an enemy, was to write the person's name on a piece of paper, wrap the paper round a stone and drop it into the water.

The curse was considered to last as long as the paper remained in the well, so people who had been ill-wished in this manner paid the well-keeper to remove their names. In 1831 a keeper was imprisoned for taking money under false pretences, and in 1929 the offending well was finally covered over.

The Husband Killer

Llannefydd, Clwyd

KATHERYN TUDOR, who lived at Llannefydd in the 16th century, had so many descendants that she was known as the 'Mother of Wales'.

She was reputed to have been married seven times and to have murdered all her husbands by pouring molten lead into their ears.

One of the unfortunate spouses must have resisted, because a wall at ancient Berain Manor – Katheryn's home – is still stained with his blood.

The Demon

Llangollen, Clwyd

ONE NIGHT Collen, a monk living in the sixth century, was visited by a messenger with a pressing invitation to the palace of Gwyn ap Nudd, who called himself the Fairy King.

Now Collen knew that Gwyn was, in fact, a demon and managed to conceal a small bottle of holy water in his robes before leaving.

He was taken to a magnificent castle in a meadow and greeted by Gwyn, who welcomed him to the 'palace of the beautiful people' and invited him to feast with them. The other guests – young men and women – were indeed beautiful, but the feast consisted of dead and decaying rushes and green pondslime in which tiny creatures wriggled.

Angrily, Collen refused to touch this disgusting fare, whereupon the 'Fairy King' drew a long sword and lunged at him. But the monk was prepared, and quickly threw the holy water into the demon's face. Gwyn ap Nudd gave one scream and then he, the other guests and the castle all vanished completely.

Collen returned home to be proclaimed a hero and a saint. Llangollen, which was named after him, means 'St Collen's Church'.

Left: View near Llangollen.
Right: Dinas Bran, Vale of Llangollen.

The Hill of Goblins

Mold, Clwyd

NEAR MOLD, there was once a hill known as Bryn yr Ellyllon – the 'Hill of the Goblins'. It had a reputation for being haunted, and many people reported having seen a ghostly figure in the vicinity.

An old woman returning to Mold late one evening was confronted by a figure of unusual size 'clothed in a coat of gold which shone like the sun'. The apparition crossed the road in front of her and disappeared into the Hill of Goblins. She was so unnerved by the experience that she hurried straight to the house of the local vicar and told him what she had seen.

Some time later, in 1833, the hill was being cleared by workmen who discovered the skeleton of a tall man laid out at full length and wearing a cloak of embossed gold. The cape had been made in the early Bronze Age, about 1400BC, but the workmen were unaware of the importance of their find, and it was broken up and the fragments were dispersed.

Fortunately, some of the pieces were recovered and reconstructed by the British Museum, where they can be seen today.

The Lost Ring

St Asaph, Llanelwy, Clwyd

THE SMALLEST cathedral in Britain takes its name from a sixth century monk, St Asaph. He was reputed to have performed many miracles, and the young wife of King Maelgwn of North Wales hoped he could perform one for her.

She called upon him in great distress because she had lost a precious ring while swimming in the river. The ring had been a gift given to her by Maelgwn, and not only was it valuable, but also traditionally worn by every queen of North Wales. Asaph invited the royal couple to dine with him the following evening, and when they arrived he told Maelgwn what had happened. But the king refused to believe his wife's story, and angrily accused her of having given the ring away.

He was still angry and upset when they sat down to supper, although somewhat appeased by the excellent fish that was served. Asaph told them it had been caught in the River Elwy earlier that day.

As soon as the king cut into his fish, the lost ring fell out on his plate. Maelgwn immediately forgave his wife, and the young wife later thanked Asaph for his miracle.

Right: St Asaph Cathedral.
Left: Sunset over the Clwydian Range.

The Beheading

Well of St Winifred, Holywell, Clwyd

WINIFRED, a beautiful young woman who lived in the seventh century, had chosen a religious vocation and taken a vow of chastity. But Caradoc, the son of a local chieftain, was unwilling to respect her vow and constantly made advances to her – which she rejected.

One day, after he had been drinking heavily, he waylaid the girl and tried to rape her. She resisted so vigorously that Caradoc, incensed, drew his sword and cut off her head.

Winifred's guardian, St Beuno, performed the miracle of restoring her head to her body.

Apparently Winifred lived for many years after this experience, and later became Abbess of Gwytherin.

Water sprang from the place where her head had fallen to the ground, and it became known as St Winifred's Well – which is how Holywell got its name.

A curse put on Caradoc's relatives by St Beuno caused the whole clan to bark like dogs, and they could only be cured by the waters of the well. To this day, St Winifred's Well is said to cure many ailments and is supposed to be particularly effective for nervous disorders.

The Horse Sprinkling

St George, Clwyd

THE VILLAGE of St George was much frequented by horse lovers. The water from the village well was said to have been blessed by St George, the patron saint of horses, and a mere sprinkling of it would preserve the animal's good health or cure it of any sickness.

In fact, so powerful were the properties of the water, that even if you had several horses it was only necessary to sprinkle one of them!

Right: The hills and valleys are steeped in mystery.

The Abbot's Vision

Valle Crucis Abbey, Clwyd

OWEN GLENDOWER, the Welsh hero who led a rebellion against English rule in 1404, disappeared mysteriously following his defeat some years later.

Shortly after his disappearance he was seen one morning by the abbot of Valle Crucis Abbey, near Llangollen. Glendower remarked that the abbot was up early. 'It is you who are up early, my lord Owen,' the abbot replied, recognizing him, 'almost a hundred years too early!'

A prophetic vision to the later rising of the Tudor dynasty, to whom Glendower was related.

Above: Visions and prophecies abound in Clwyd.

Legends from Powys

The Fairy Door

Brecon Beacons, Powys

Above: Arthur's Stone, Hay on Wye, Powys.
Below: Pen y Fan, in the beautiful Brecon Beacons.

ABOVE VALLEYS carved by Ice Age glaciers loom the Brecon Beacons, where King Arthur is said to have assembled the followers who became the Knights of the Round Table. The dip between the peaks of Pen y Fan and Corn Du is known as 'Arthur's Chair'.

Legend says that there was once a secret fairy door in the Beacons, near the lake called Llym Cwm Llwch. This legendary door was opened every year on May Day to admit mortals to Fairyland. The custom continued until one visitor was ungracious enough to steal a flower from a fairy, and the door has never been opened to a mortal since.

Some years after the final closing of the fairy door, the people of Brecon decided to drain Llyn Cwm Llwch. Valuable treasure was believed to lie at the bottom of the lake and they were eager to get their hands on it.

They had barely begun the task before a giant emerged from the water. Towering above them, he threatened to drown their town and all the land around the River Wye if they did not leave him in peace. No one argued – and the lake was never drained!

Right: Builth Wells, where the pawprint of King Arthurs hunting dog could be seen.

Below: Pen y Fan mountain and Pontsticill Reservoir.

The 'Carn of Cabal'

Builth Wells, Powys

MANY YEARS ago Builth Wells was known as 'Buelt', and at that time it was reputed to be the site of 'Carn Cabal' – a heap of stone's marked by the pawprint of King Arthur's hunting dog, Cabal.

What Arthur and his dog were hunting when the print was left on the stone is unclear, but legend suggests that it could have been the legendary boar, Twrch Trwyth.

The boar had a magic comb between its ears, and this comb was needed by a giant to untangle his hair. Arthur was hunting Twrch Trwyth to obtain the magic comb for a young man who wished to marry the giant's daughter.

Twrch Trwyth and his piglets were hunted from Ireland, across Wales – where all the piglets were killed – and on to Cornwall, in England. Here the magic comb was finally won and the boar driven into the sea, never to return.

The hunt may well have passed through Buelt, where Arthur placed Cabal's stone on top of the cairn. The stone had magic properties, and whenever it was removed it always returned mysteriously to 'Cabal's Carn'.

The Shrinking Bull

Hyssington, Powys

MANY YEARS ago, the parish of Hyssington was terrorized by a huge bull. It was said that the creature had been an evil squire who was turned into a bull by a magician. But the bull was even more evil than the squire, and the villagers asked the parson of Hyssington to rid them of the menace.

The parson confronted the animal and read to it from the Bible, and as he preached, the bull began to shrink. So he led it into the church and preached to it until nightfall, by which time it was scarcely larger than a cat.

When the parson's candle burnt out he had to stop preaching, and immediately the bull began to grow again – and went on growing until it filled the entire church.

At first light the parson started to preach again and, gradually, the bull began to shrink once more. He continued to preach throughout the day, and by evening the bull was small enough to pick up and drop into one of his boots.

The parson buried the boot – with the bull inside it – beneath the step by the church door, where it has remained ever since.

Above: Llanthony Priory near Abergavenny.

Above: The spectacular snow-capped Brecon Beacons.

The Sunken City

Llangorse Lake, Powys

BENEATH Llangorse Lake – Llyn Syfaddan – there is said to be a drowned city. The land once belonged to a beautiful princess who was courted by a young man with very little money.

She told him she could only marry him if he brought her riches. Desperate for her love, the young man robbed and murdered a wealthy merchant and took the money to the princess.

She accepted it and they were married. But the merchant's ghost haunted them, warning them that their crime would be avenged on the ninth generation of their family. The princess ignored the threat. 'By that time we shall be in our graves,' she told her husband. 'Let us enjoy the money while we may.'

The couple lived to a be great age, and years afterwards they invited their many descendants to a feast. At the height of the celebration, they were all swallowed up by a terrible earthquake and covered over by the lake.

It is said that on certain days the city can still be seen below the waters of Llangorse Lake – and that sometimes the sound of the church bells may be heard.

Left: It is said that the lake still hides it's secrets.

Moll Walbee's Stone

Llowes, Powys

A LARGE, FLAT, upright stone with a wheelcross on one side used to stand in Llowes churchyard. This is Moll Walbee's Stone, and it has now been placed inside the church.

Moll Walbee was a legendary giantess who built Hay Castle in a night. The stone either fell from her apron as she passed Llowes, or she felt it in her shoe and hurled it angrily across the Wye from Hay.

There are many tales told of Moll Walbee, or Malld Walbri, who seems to have been quite a tyrant in the 12th century. She was, in fact, a real person and the wife of William de Braose, a baron who built Colwyn Castle.

Moll herself successfully defended the castle against attack in 1195, and was described as being 'shrewd, stout and stomackfull'.

It is also possible that Moll was the legendary *Mallt y Nos*, 'Matilda of the Night'. When rebuked for her love of hunting, Matilda replied that she found the sport preferable to the thought of heaven. She was immediately condemned to join the Hounds of Hell, and to travel forever through the air with them on stormy nights.

Right: The Brecon Beacons – both beautiful and mysterious throughout the seasons.

Melangell and the Hare

Pennant Melangell, Powys

ONE DAY, a prince of Powys was hunting with his hounds when they gave chase to a hare. The hare tracked cleverly from side to side of the meadow and then ran into the forest, with the hounds very close behind. The chase was intense and the hare soon became exhausted.

The prince followed his hounds into the forest on horseback, and saw that the hare had taken shelter between the feet of a young woman.

Despite all his urging, not one of the dogs would approach it for the kill. He asked the young woman her name and she said it was Melangell, and that she had come from Ireland to worship in the tranquillity of Pennant. The prince realized that he was in the presence of a saint, and offered Melangell the land and means to build a chapel.

She became the patron saint of hares, and in the district of Pennant the animals are sometimes called *wym bach Melangell*, 'Melangell's little lambs'.

The saint's meeting with the prince is shown by 15th century wood-carvings on a screen in the Norman church at Pennant Melangell.

Right: The Pennant Valley in the Cambrian Mountains.

Legends of Dyfed

The Monster's Grave

Bedd-yr-Afanc, Dyfed

ACROSS THE moor from the village of Brynberian is Bedd-yr-Afanc, the 'Monster's Grave', sometimes also known as the 'Monster's Mound'. The 'monster' was an afanc, captured in a pool near Brynberian bridge and buried in the grave on the mountainside.

How the afanc was caught remains a mystery, although it is likely that Hu Gadarn, who dragged an afanc from the pool above Betws-y-Coed, also employed his two great horned oxen to assist in the removal of this particular beast.

Once, an afanc lived in Llyn Barfog, the 'Bearded Lake', and caused it to break its banks and flood the land. Everyone was said to have drowned save one man and one woman, from whom Wales was peopled again.

Hu Gadarn – 'Hu the Mighty' as he was known – used his two great oxen to drag the afanc out of the lake and on to dry land, so that such a disaster could not be repeated.

No one seemed to know exactly what sort of beast the afanc was. Descriptions varied from a 'water-dwelling ogre' to a 'dragon-like creature' that lurked in caves – with a poisoned spear at the ready to kill anyone who approached.

Left: This ancient monument at Pentre Ifan, is close to the village of Brynberian where the afanc once lived.

Ceridwen the Witch

Borth, Dyfed

CERIDWEN THE witch had made a secret potion that would give knowledge to any who drank it. But no sooner had she poured it from her cauldron before it was stolen and swallowed by a man called Gwion Bach.

Ceridwen gave chase, but as she approached Gwion he turned into a hare. She countered this by turning into a greyhound, gaining on him rapidly as they raced along a river-bank. But Gwion turned into a fish and flopped into the water.

The witch turned into an otter and dived in after him, whereupon he arose from the river as a bird, and flew away. She then hunted him as a hawk and he, thinking to fool her at last, became a grain of wheat. But she turned into a hen and ate him.

Nine months later Ceridwen gave birth to a baby boy – the legendary 6th century poet, Taliesin. She cast him into the sea in a cradle, which was washed ashore near Borth.

It was found by King Gwyddno of the now drowned land of Cantref Gwaelod. He named the boy Taliesin, meaning 'beautiful brow' – a fitting name for a future poet.

Right: Whitesand bay at St David's Head.

Merlin's City

Carmarthen, Dyfed

CARMARTHEN IS very much 'Merlin's City'. The Welsh name is Caerfyrddrin, meaning the town of Myrddin – or Merlin.

Merlin's tree – an ancient oak – used to stand in the town centre and had a prophecy attached to it:

'When Myrddin's tree shall tumble down,
Then shall fall Carmarthen town.'

However, increased traffic overcame tradition, and in 1978 the carefully preserved tree became an obstruction and was uprooted. The remains are now in Carmarthen Museum at Abergwili.

Bryn Myrddin, 'Merlin's Hill', is just outside Carmarthen and according to one legend the immortal magician still remains imprisoned in a cave there.

Merlin fell in love with Viviane, a lake-maiden, and as they travelled together desire made him incautious, and he revealed many of his magic secrets. Viviane was a good listener, and when she grew tired of Merlin she used a magic spell to imprison him in a cave on the lower part of the hill. There he remains, held in her bonds of enchantment for ever.

Some people say that if you listen in the right place on Bryn Myrddin, you can hear his groans. But others prefer to think of him still sleeping on Bardsey Island.

The Drowned Land

Cardigan Bay, Dyfed

BELOW THE waters of Cardigan Bay is the legendary drowned land of Cantref Gwaelod.

The land and its cities were protected from the encroaching sea by a series of banks and sluices, and it was the job of the keeper of the embankment to shut the sluice gates every night.

One night, in a drunken stupor, he forgot to do so. The sea overwhelmed the land and few of the inhabitants survived.

The Devil's Bridge

Bryn Garv, Dyfed

BELOW BRYN GARV, three bridges cross the River Mynarch where it flows through a deep gorge, and the first of these bridges was built by the Devil.

An old woman's cow had become stranded on the other side of the gorge, and the Devil promised to build her a bridge if he could take the first living thing to cross it. The old woman's son was due shortly, and the Devil knew it. But she agreed, and the bridge was built.

The son came into view and the Devil chuckled gleefully. But the old woman quickly threw a piece of bread across the bridge and her dog ran after it. Frustrated, the Devil had to claim the dog.

Left: The view from Devil's Bridge.

Right: The dramatic coastline of Cardigan Bay.

The Fairy Wife

Llyn y Fan Fach, Dyfed

ONCE UPON a magical-time, a beautiful girl sat on the banks of Llyn y Fan Fach, the 'Little Lake of the Fan'. She was a fairy, who had come from the dark waters of the lake to comb her hair in the sunshine.

A young farmer called Gwyn was grazing his cattle on the banks of the lake, and saw the girl. Immediately, he fell passionately in love with her and begged her to marry him.

At first the water-fairy refused him, but eventually she agreed to become his wife. She warned him, however, that he would only be allowed to strike her twice during their marriage – for at the third blow she would vanish for ever.

The girl's father gave her a dowry of fairy sheep, cattle and horses and the young couple were married. For many years they lived happily on a farm just outside Myddfai, and the fairy bore three fine sons.

One day, she was day-dreaming of her beautiful lake, and her husband tapped her smartly on the shoulder to regain her attention. She paled, for unintentionally he had struck her for the first time.

Some months later, the farmer and his fairy wife were at a wedding when she suddenly burst into tears. Gwyn patted her on the shoulder and asked why she wept.

'I am weeping because the young couple's troubles are just beginning,' she said, 'and so are ours – for you have just struck the second blow!'

Above: Sea mist and heather on the Pembrokeshire coast.

Right: Llyn y Fan Fach, the lake of the little fairy.

After that, the farmer was particularly careful not to 'strike' his wife again, until one day she started laughing at a funeral. He gave her a quick tap on the arm and asked her to stop.

'When mortals die, their troubles end,' she said, 'and so must our marriage – for that was the third blow!'

The fairy returned to the lake, taking her animals with her. She called each one by name: 'Hump-brindled, Rump-brindled, Squint-eyed, Dappled-hide' – and so forth. They all disappeared beneath the waters of Llyn y Fan Fach and the farmer never saw his fairy wife again.

However, she appeared to her sons from time to time, to instruct them in the use of herbal medicines. All three became physicians at the nearby village of Myddfai and their descendants were still physicians to the 19th century. Some of their ancient herbal remedies even survive to this day.

The Fairy Islands

Milford Haven, Dyfed

THE GREEN Islands of the Sea – the invisible country of the fairies – lie somewhere off Milford Haven. Sailors still spoke of these 'green meadows of enchantment' in the last century.

Some even went ashore on them, to see them suddenly vanish when they returned to their boats. The fairies who inhabited the Green Islands shopped regularly at the markets in Milford Haven. They never spoke, yet always seemed to get what they required. They would pay the correct money and then depart in silence.

The Green Islands could sometimes be seen from Milford Haven, and it was thought the fairies went back and forth through a secret underwater tunnel.

Hunting the Wren

Marloes, Dyfed

IN THE vicinity of Marloes, the pagan custom of 'Hunting the Wren' survived until the end of the 19th century. The bird was considered to embody the evils of winter, and the hunting took place around Twelfth Night.

When the wren was captured, it was placed in a wooden 'wren-house', and carried round the town by men who sang of their willingness to sell the bird in order to buy beer. The singers were welcomed into every house and given money or drink.

Above Right: The beach at Newgale, St. Brides Bay.
Right: Marloes Sands, the site of ancient pagan customs.

The Viper

Roch y Garn (near Haverfordwest), Dyfed

ROCH CASTLE stands alone on a rocky outcrop, high above the surrounding land. Adam de la Roche, a 13th century lord of Roch, was told by a witch that a viper would cause his death. However, if he could manage to survive one given year in safety, he need never again fear the serpent.

De la Roche ordered a castle to be built that would be beyond the reach of any snake, and so Roch Castle was constructed in its present position.

At the beginning of the given year Adam de la Roche moved into the top floor of the castle. And there he stayed, fearful and watchful, for the whole year. Finally, only one day remained before he would be released from the witch's prophecy. De la Roche began to relax, feeling confident that he had outwitted fate.

It was bitterly cold, and someone sent a basket of firewood into the castle, so that his last night in isolation would be warm and comfortable. But as Adam de la Roche piled the logs on to the fire, a serpent crawled from the basket and bit him, killing him almost instantly.

Left: The 'Green Bridge of Wales' on the rugged Pembrokeshire coast.

Legends of the Patron Saint

St David's, Dyfed

NOTHING NOW remains of the monasteries founded in the 6th century by St David, or – in Welsh – Dewi Sant. But the tiny cathedral city on the peninsula remains and St David's, or Dewisland, has been a place of pilgrimage for over a thousand years.

St Non's Bay, half a mile from the cathedral, was one of the landing places for pilgrims. It was here that David (or Dewi) was born to a Welsh girl called Non, at the height of a raging storm.

St David was often called the Waterman, possibly because he and his monks abstained from alcohol. A number of Irish saints are said to have been taught by him, so he may well have influenced the spread of Christianity in Ireland.

St Patrick is reputed to have come to the peninsula to settle, some 30 years before David was born. But he had a dream of Ireland, in which an angel bade him return – telling him that this place was already reserved for the Welsh saint.

The area where David built his monastery was terrorized by an Irish brigand named Boia, whose shrewish wife urged him to get rid of the monks.

However, much to the wife's annoyance. David managed to tame the wild Irishman, Determined to cause trouble she sent her maidservants naked to the monastery, hoping they would tempt the monks to break their vows of chastity. But following David's example of self-control they were able to resist the young women's charms. The girls returned to their mistress feeling rebuked – and probably very cold.

David became the most prominent leader of the new Celtic church. His discipline was rigid but his manner gentle, and he soon acquired a great many disciples. He was also reputed to have performed a number of miracles.

There was no water near his monastery, and as he prayed one day a well suddenly appeared by his feet. Many other holy wells are associated with

Above: Ancient rocks at St. David's Head.
Right: Skomer Island, now a nature reserve, seen from St. Brides Bay.

Above: St. David's Cathedral is still a place of pilgrimage.
Left: Dramatic rocks on the coast at Abereiddi.

St David. The Physician's Well near Aberaeron sprang from the ground at the place where he had healed the blind and the sick, and the holy well of St Non's, at St David's, is also credited with healing powers.

David died on March 1st, 580AD, and March 1st has been 'St David's Day' – the National Day of Wales – ever since.

The Ringing Rock

St Govan's Chapel, Dyfed

THE TINY chapel of St Govan is perched on a rocky ledge above the sea, a mile south of Bosherston.

The chapel – part of which may date from the fifth century – is reached by a flight of stone steps. There are 52 steps, but they never count the same going up as going down!

The little bell-cote above the entrance is empty now, but it once held a silver bell that was stolen by pirates. Sea-nymphs rescued it and, unable to reach the bell-cote, placed it on a nearby rock. The bell has long since gone – but find the rock and it will ring when you strike it.

Inside the chapel is a vertical cleft in the rock-face, said to have opened miraculously to conceal St Govan from his enemies. Yet just who St Govan was remains a mystery. Some claim that he was a disciple of St David. Others maintain that he was really Sir Gawaine, one of the Knights of the Round Table, who became a hermit after the death of King Arthur.

St Govan's well, just below the chapel, is said to have the healing power to cure afflictions of the eye.

Below: The tiny chapel of St.Govan.

Beset by Disasters

Strata Florida Abbey, Dyfed

STEEP HILLS look down on the ruins of Strata Florida Abbey, once a centre of holiness, learning and toil.

In 1164 the Cistercian monks first settled in Strata Florida, which was their name for Ystrad Fflur – the 'Vale of Flowers'. But the abbey seemed beset by disasters. Lightning struck it in 1285 and caused great damage, and ten years later Edward I set fire to it because it was a stronghold of Welsh nationalism.

Early in the 15th century it suffered further damage when it became a garrison for Henry IV's troops during the fight for Welsh independence. The abbey was closed by order of Henry VIII, and only the outline of the ground plan and an arch at the west door now remain.

Although the monks left Strata Florida centuries ago, their spirits still linger on. There have been reports of candles blazing among the ruins, and on Christmas Eve the ghostly figure of a monk has been seen, busily trying to rebuild the altar.

Left: The rocky cliffs are said to have provided St. Govan with a secret and magical hiding place.

The Women in Red

Strumble Head, Fishguard, Dyfed

FEBRUARY 22nd 1797 was the date of the last foreign invasion of British soil – and it didn't go at all as planned!

An American officer called Tate led a French expeditionary force which landed at Strumble Head. Tate had hoped to effect a peasants' rebellion, but his troops proved to be a great disappointment to him.

His choice of men had been limited and they were mostly ex-convicts. They set up headquarters in a cellar and stole drink from the inns and looted the local farms. The men of the district formed their own small army, but they were powerless against the wild Frenchmen.

Jemima Nicholas was less easily daunted, however. She and several other women donned red cloaks and advanced on the drunken French soldiers. Lord Cawdor had now brought in the Castlemartin Yeomanry, but the Frenchmen fled in terror as soon as they saw the women in red – mistaking them for the British army.

The French soldiers surrendered to Lord Cawdor on February 24th. Jemima Nicholas, who became known as the 'General of the Red Army', died in 1832 and is buried at St Mary's Church in Fishguard.

Right: Fishguard Bay with Dinas Head in background.

'Denbigh of the Fish'

Tenby, Dyfed

IN WELSH, Tenby is called Dinbych-y-Pysgod, 'Denbigh of the Fish', to distinguish it from Dinbych (Denbigh) in Clwyd.

The 12th century castle and massive town walls – built two centuries later – were planned to make Tenby impregnable to an enemy. But in 1644, Cromwell's bombardment by land and from the sea caused the town to fall to the Parliamentarians.

In the 19th century Tenby was developed as a watering place by Sir William Paxton, designer of the famous Crystal Palace. Laston House, by the harbour, was built by Paxton specifically for seawater baths, and bears a Greek inscription that translates as: 'The sea washes away the ills of man.'

An old Tenby tradition that has survived is associated not with washing, but with sprinkling. On New Year's Day the local children sprinkle passing townsfolk with fresh raindrops from twigs of box-thorn or holly. And if the season is dry, presumably they have ways of improvising! It is certainly considered lucky to be sprinkled, and the children are usually rewarded with money.

The custom of sprinkling probably dates back to pagan purification rites, but by the Middle Ages it had become a Christian practice and was associated with the Virgin Mary.

Below Left: The picturesque harbour at Tenby.
Below: Waterfall on the beach at Tresaith.

The Highwayman's Lesson

Ystrad-ffyn, Dyfed

A 16th CENTURY OUTLAW called Twm had a cave near Ystrad-ffyn as his hideout. While his reputation was such that many had cause to fear him, Twm abhorred unnecessary violence. He was angered by the behaviour of another local highwayman, who was known to be cruel and greedy.

Twm decided the time had come to teach this fellow a lesson. So he disguised himself as a poor farmer and mounted a tired old nag, whose saddle-bags he had filled with stones.

He rode to a place where he knew the other highwayman lay in ambush, and ambled past on his old nag. Instantly, the cruel outlaw leapt out of hiding and levelled a couple of pistols at him.

Twm put up a fine pretence of being terrified and began to give up his belongings as he had been ordered. But instead of handing over the saddle-bags meekly, he hurled them over a hedge and into a field.

The highwayman scrambled after them and, while he was picking them up, Twm leapt from his own nag on to the other man's horse. He galloped away, chuckling – for he had acquired a beautiful mare whose saddle-bags were already filled with stolen money.

The Toll Wreckers

Yr Efail Wen, Dyfed

MANY TOLL-GATES appeared on the roads of South Wales in the first part of the 19th century. The farmers objected to this extra financial burden, and decided to take the law into their own hands. The men disguised themselves as women – so that if they were seen they would not be suspected of violence – and attacked the gates by night.

There were many of these gangs, and their leader was always called 'Rebecca'. This possibly reflected a passage from Genesis, in the Bible: 'And they blessed Rebekah and said . . . let thy seed possess the gate of those which hate them.'

Sometimes 'Rebecca' would appear as an old blind woman, pausing at the gate and saying, 'O my children – something is in my way!' And the rest of the gang would promptly remove the obstacle for her by tearing the gate down.

The first toll-gate to be destroyed was at Yr Efail Wen, and 'Rebecca' was a huge man called Tom Rees. Many other gates were subsequently destroyed by the 'Rebecca' gangs and finally, in 1844, the authorities removed all the offending obstacles officially.

Right: Pembroke Castle – an imposing sight at sunset.
Left: The ruins of Carreg Cennen Castle.

Legends of the South

King Arthur's Cave

Craig-y-Dinas, West Glamorgan

ACCORDING to tradition, Craig-y-Ddinas – the Rock of the Fortress – was the rock from which Merlin persuaded King Arthur to draw the sword Excalibur.

The Craig y Dinas Cave, near Glyn Neath, is also one of several places where Arthur and his knights are said to be sleeping.

A magician once discovered the secret whereabouts of a hidden tunnel leading to the cave. He enlisted the help of a farmer to dig a way into the tunnel, promising him a share of the treasure in return for his labour.

The tunnel led to a large cave with a bell at the entrance. Inside, King Arthur and his knights were sleeping, surrounded by piles of gold. The magician told the farmer to take as much of the treasure as he could carry, but on no account to return for more.

But the farmer disobeyed the magician's warning and returned for more gold the following day. The moment he touched the

Above: The ruins of Ogmore Castle, near Porthcawl on the south Wales Coast.

treasure the bell at the cave entrance rang loudly and the knights awoke.

A great gust of wind then hurled the farmer outside, injuring his legs so badly that he was crippled for life. He never found the cave, or the tunnel again.

Above: There are still knights in shining armour at Chepstow Castle.

Jack O'Kent

Grosmont, Gwent

GROSMONT, on the Welsh border, was once the home of Jack O'Kent, a famous Welsh wizard.

Jack and the Devil were ever trying to outwit each other in trials of strength and cunning. One day, Jack took the Devil into a field of corn that was just sprouting. 'Which will you have?' he asked him, 'the tops or the butts?'

There was not much to be seen of the tops, so the Devil chose the butts, or bottoms. When harvest came, Jack got the wheat and the Devil was left with the straw.

On another occasion Jack and the Devil agreed to have a hay mowing contest. But the night before, Jack scattered the Devil's half of the meadow with metal harrow tines.

Throughout the contest the Devil had to stop to sharpen his scythe. As he did so he was heard to mutter, 'Bur-doch, Jack! Bur-doch!' obviously mistaking the tines for the coarse burdock plant. Jack won the contest – although the Devil does seem to have been less astute than usual!

Jack O'Kent's grave is said to be marked by an old cross on the north side of Grosmont churchyard.

Left: Chepstow Castle.

The First Cremation

Llantrisant, Mid Glamorgan

DR WILLIAM PRICE was a well-known 19th century eccentric who lived at Llantrisant. He would perform Druid ceremonies at the Rocking Stone on Pontypridd Common – often wearing a fox skin on his head.

Price outlived his son, who died in 1884. Spurning burial or a Christian ceremony, he burnt the body in a field near his home. This caused a local outcry and he was arrested for his 'crime' and tried at Cardiff.

Dr Price maintained that he was acting within his rights – and despite strong opposition he won his case. He could be considered the 'pioneer' of cremation, as it was made legal shortly afterwards.

Fairy Revels

Panmaen, West Glamorgan

PENNARD CASTLE is now a ruin, lying in the sand dunes on the Gower Peninsula. It was once owned by Lord Rhys, who married the beautiful daughter of a prince of North Wales.

On the wedding night there was great revelry in the castle. But outside, the sentries became aware of sweeter, ethereal music close by. Then they saw the fairies – dancing on the grass in the moonlight, just inside the castle gates.

Lord Rhys ordered his men to drive the fairies away. His new wife was horrified, and warned him that such an action would bring dreadful misfortune to them all. Lord Rhys replied haughtily that he was afraid of no one, mortal or fairy. He took his bravest men and went out to do battle with the fairies. But the little people vanished as he approached, and not one of them was harmed.

A voice was heard on the night air. 'You have spoilt our innocent sport,' it cried, 'and now your proud castle shall be spoilt.' Instantly, a terrible sandstorm blew over the castle, burying it and all its occupants.

The Last Run

Llanwonno, Mid Glamorgan

GRIFFITH MORGAN is buried at Llanwonno. He lived from 1700-1737 and was considered the greatest runner in Wales.

He could speed across a nearby mountain in the time it took to boil a kettle. It was said that he paced himself against hares and slept in a dung-pile to strengthen his legs.

In 1737, having just run 12 miles in record time, he was slapped on the back by an admirer and died of heart failure.

Left: The breathtaking beauty of Caerphilly Castle.

Legends of the Mines

Port Talbot, West Glamorgan

SUPERSTITION was rife in the coal mines of south Wales, and many strange tales were told by the miners that seemed to justify their belief in the supernatural.

Birds flying around the pithead were considered ominous – robins, pigeons and doves being particular harbingers of doom. They were known as 'corpse birds' and were said to have been seen before the explosion at Senghennydd Colliery in 1913, when 400 miners died.

At Morfa Colliery, near Port Talbot, many uncanny incidents were reported during the early months of 1890. The colliery was filled with an overwhelmingly sweet smell, said to come from the invisible 'death flowers' that gave off their aroma before a disaster. Flickering lights – called 'corpse candles' – appeared in the tunnels. The ghosts of dead miners were seen at the pit-face, and ghostly cries for help were heard.

So persistent were these manifestations that on March 10th almost half the workers on the morning shift stayed at home. Later that day there was an explosion at the colliery, and more than 80 miners who had turned up for work were buried alive and perished in the disaster.

Right: The Rhymney Valley, South Wales.

Arthur's Stone

Reynoldston, West Glamorgan

ON CEFN BRYN Common, on the Gower Peninsula, stands 'Arthur's Stone'. It is said to be the 'pebble' that King Arthur removed from his boot on his way to the battle of Camlann in AD539. He threw it over his shoulder and it landed seven miles away, on the common near Reynoldston.

Local girls used to place a honey cake soaked in milk on the stone at midnight, when the moon was full. They would then walk three times round the stone, and if their lovers were true they would join the girls on the common.

The Red Castle

Tongwynlais, South Glamorgan

THE PRESENT Castle Coch – the Red Castle – was built on the foundations of a stronghold dating from the 12th century.

The old castle belonged to Ifor Bach who had a small army of 1200 men. But he claimed that his men were more than a match for any army ten times greater than they were.

Ifor's treasure still lies beneath Castle Coch, hidden in a deep vault guarded by three huge eagles. The birds will continue to watch over the treasure until Ifor and his 1200 brave men return to claim it.

Above and right: Castle Coch, the Red Castle. Legend says that hidden treasure is guarded by three huge eagles.

The Tiny People

Vale of Neath, West Glamorgan

THE VALE of Neath, where the Rock of Fortune stands, was once the haunt of fairies. And the rock itself – Craig-y-Ddinas – was said to be their fortress.

In those far off fairy days a boy called Elidyr ran away from home. Although he loved his mother dearly, his tutor was so harsh that he could stand it no longer. He stayed hidden under the hollow bank of a river for two days, without anything to eat.

On the evening of the second day, a tiny man appeared and said he would take the boy to a land that was 'all playtime and pleasure'. Elidyr agreed to go with him, and the fairy led him through an underground passage to a beautiful land of meadows and rivers.

Here the tiny folk ate neither meat nor fish, and lived on junket. They rode horses no bigger than greyhounds – and never told lies. Elidyr made friends with the king's son – a boy of his own age – and they would play together with a golden ball.

The days passed happily and the mortal boy grew to love the tiny people and their enchanted country. He often returned to the upper world to visit his mother and the fairies never objected.

Then one day she asked him to bring home some of the fairies' gold and Elidyr stole the golden ball. But he was seen by the fairy folk, and as he ran home he found himself hotly pursued by two of the tiny people.

He had just reached the threshold of his house when he tripped and fell, and the ball slipped from his grasp. It rolled towards the two tiny men who snatched it up and turned on their heels without a word, plainly showing their contempt for his action.

Elidyr was now consumed with shame. He got to his feet and retraced his steps to the river-bank and the secret passage, intending to apologize to the fairies and beg their forgiveness. But when he came to the place where the passage had been, he was unable to find the entrance.

Above: Three Cliffs Bay on the Gower Peninsular.   *Right: Winter sunset on Rudry Common, near Caerphilly.*

Index & Place Names